MW01172634

Meet		Date	Level	Age Div

Event	Score	Place
Vault		
Bars		
Beam		
Floor		
All Around		

I HAD A NO FALL MEET!

YEAH ME!   WHOOPS

My Team Did Great Too!

My Team Placed

Name	Vault	Bars	Beam	Floor	A.A.

The FUNNIEST thing happened . . .	The HIGHLIGHT was . . .

I Feel like I did . . .	V	UB	BB	FX
THE BEST EVER!				
Better than last time				
OK, The same				
ugh, I'll do better next time				

Photo Op!

For the next meet I'm going to work on . . .

Meet		Date	Level	Age Div

Event	Score	Place
Vault		
Bars		
Beam		
Floor		
All Around		

I HAD A NO FALL MEET!

YEAH ME!   WHOOPS

My Team Did Great Too!

My Team Placed

Name	Vault	Bars	Beam	Floor	A.A.

The FUNNIEST thing happened . . .	The HIGHLIGHT was . . .

I Feel like I did . . .	V	UB	BB	FX
THE BEST EVER!				
Better than last time				
OK, The same				
ugh, I'll do better next time				

Photo Op!

For the next meet I'm going to work on . . .

Meet		Date	Level	Age Div

Event	Score	Place
Vault		
Bars		
Beam		
Floor		
All Around		

I HAD A NO FALL MEET!

YEAH ME!   WHOOPS

My Team Did Great Too!

My Team Placed

Name	Vault	Bars	Beam	Floor	A.A.

The FUNNIEST thing happened . . .	The HIGHLIGHT was . . .

I Feel like I did . . .	V	UB	BB	FX
THE BEST EVER!				
Better than last time				
OK, The same				
ugh, I'll do better next time				

Photo Op!

For the next meet I'm going to work on . . .

Meet			Date	Level	Age Div

Event	Score	Place
Vault		
Bars		
Beam		
Floor		
All Around		

I HAD A NO FALL MEET!

YEAH ME!   WHOOPS

My Team Did Great Too!

My Team Placed

Name	Vault	Bars	Beam	Floor	A.A.

The FUNNIEST thing happened . . .	The HIGHLIGHT was . . .

I Feel like I did . . .	V	UB	BB	FX
THE BEST EVER!				
Better than last time				
OK, The same				
ugh, I'll do better next time				

Photo Op!

For the next meet I'm going to work on . . .

Meet		Date	Level	Age Div

Event	Score	Place
Vault		
Bars		
Beam		
Floor		
All Around		

I HAD A NO FALL MEET!

YEAH ME!   WHOOPS

My Team Did Great Too!

My Team Placed

Name	Vault	Bars	Beam	Floor	A.A.

The FUNNIEST thing happened . . .	The HIGHLIGHT was . . .

I Feel like I did . . .	V	UB	BB	FX
THE BEST EVER!				
Better than last time				
OK, The same				
ugh, I'll do better next time				

Photo Op!

For the next meet I'm going to work on . . .

Meet		Date	Level	Age Div

Event	Score	Place
Vault		
Bars		
Beam		
Floor		
All Around		

I HAD A NO FALL MEET!

YEAH ME!   WHOOPS

My Team Placed

My Team Did Great Too!

Name	Vault	Bars	Beam	Floor	A.A.

The FUNNIEST thing happened . . .	The HIGHLIGHT was . . .

I Feel like I did . . .	V	UB	BB	FX
THE BEST EVER!				
Better than last time				
OK, The same				
ugh, I'll do better next time				

Photo Op!

For the next meet I'm going to work on . . .

Meet		Date	Level	Age Div

Event	Score	Place
Vault		
Bars		
Beam		
Floor		
All Around		

I HAD A NO FALL MEET!

YEAH ME!   WHOOPS

My Team Did Great Too!

My Team
Placed

Name	Vault	Bars	Beam	Floor	A.A.

The FUNNIEST thing happened . . .	The HIGHLIGHT was . . .

I Feel like I did . . .	V	UB	BB	FX
THE BEST EVER!				
Better than last time				
OK, The same				
ugh, I'll do better next time				

Photo Op!

For the next meet I'm going to work on . . .

Meet		Date	Level	Age Div

Event	Score	Place
Vault		
Bars		
Beam		
Floor		
All Around		

I HAD A NO FALL MEET!

YEAH ME!   WHOOPS

My Team Placed

My Team Did Great Too!

Name	Vault	Bars	Beam	Floor	A.A.

The FUNNIEST thing happened . . .	The HIGHLIGHT was . . .

I Feel like I did . . .	V	UB	BB	FX
THE BEST EVER!				
Better than last time				
OK, The same				
ugh, I'll do better next time				

Photo Op!

For the next meet I'm going to work on . . .

Meet		Date	Level	Age Div

Event	Score	Place
Vault		
Bars		
Beam		
Floor		
All Around		

I HAD A NO FALL MEET!

YEAH ME!   WHOOPS

My Team Did Great Too!

My Team Placed

Name	Vault	Bars	Beam	Floor	A.A.

The FUNNIEST thing happened . . .	The HIGHLIGHT was . . .

I Feel like I did . . .	V	UB	BB	FX
THE BEST EVER!				
Better than last time				
OK, The same				
ugh, I'll do better next time				

Photo Op!

For the next meet I'm going to work on . . .

Meet		Date	Level	Age Div

Event	Score	Place
Vault		
Bars		
Beam		
Floor		
All Around		

I HAD A NO FALL MEET!

YEAH ME!   WHOOPS

My Team Placed

My Team Did Great Too!

Name	Vault	Bars	Beam	Floor	A.A.

The FUNNIEST thing happened . . .	The HIGHLIGHT was . . .

I Feel like I did . . .	V	UB	BB	FX
THE BEST EVER!				
Better than last time				
OK, The same				
ugh, I'll do better next time				

Photo Op!

For the next meet I'm going to work on . . .

Meet		Date	Level	Age Div

Event	Score	Place
Vault		
Bars		
Beam		
Floor		
All Around		

I HAD A NO FALL MEET!

YEAH ME!   WHOOPS

My Team Did Great Too!

My Team Placed

Name	Vault	Bars	Beam	Floor	A.A.

The FUNNIEST thing happened . . .	The HIGHLIGHT was . . .

I Feel like I did . . .	V	UB	BB	FX
THE BEST EVER!				
Better than last time				
OK, The same				
ugh, I'll do better next time				

Photo Op!

For the next meet I'm going to work on . . .

Meet		Date	Level	Age Div

Event	Score	Place
Vault		
Bars		
Beam		
Floor		
All Around		

I HAD A NO FALL MEET!

YEAH ME!   WHOOPS

My Team Did Great Too!

My Team Placed

Name	Vault	Bars	Beam	Floor	A.A.

The FUNNIEST thing happened . . .	The HIGHLIGHT was . . .

I Feel like I did . . .	V	UB	BB	FX
THE BEST EVER!				
Better than last time				
OK, The same				
ugh, I'll do better next time				

Photo Op!

For the next meet I'm going to work on . . .

Meet		Date	Level	Age Div

Event	Score	Place
Vault		
Bars		
Beam		
Floor		
All Around		

I HAD A NO FALL MEET!

YEAH ME!   WHOOPS

My Team
Placed

My Team Did Great Too!

Name	Vault	Bars	Beam	Floor	A.A.

The FUNNIEST thing happened . . .	The HIGHLIGHT was . . .

I Feel like I did . . .	V	UB	BB	FX
THE BEST EVER!				
Better than last time				
OK, The same				
ugh, I'll do better next time				

Photo Op!

For the next meet I'm going to work on . . .

Meet		Date	Level	Age Div

Event	Score	Place
Vault		
Bars		
Beam		
Floor		
All Around		

I HAD A NO FALL MEET!

YEAH ME!   WHOOPS

My Team Did Great Too!

My Team Placed

Name	Vault	Bars	Beam	Floor	A.A.

The FUNNIEST thing happened . . .	The HIGHLIGHT was . . .

I Feel like I did . . .	V	UB	BB	FX
THE BEST EVER!				
Better than last time				
OK, The same				
ugh, I'll do better next time				

Photo Op!

For the next meet I'm going to work on . . .

Meet		Date	Level	Age Div

Event	Score	Place
Vault		
Bars		
Beam		
Floor		
All Around		

I HAD A NO FALL MEET!

YEAH ME!   WHOOPS

My Team Placed

My Team Did Great Too!

Name	Vault	Bars	Beam	Floor	A.A.

The FUNNIEST thing happened . . .	The HIGHLIGHT was . . .

I Feel like I did . . .	V	UB	BB	FX
THE BEST EVER!				
Better than last time				
OK, The same				
ugh, I'll do better next time				

Photo Op!

For the next meet I'm going to work on . . .

Meet			Date	Level	Age Div

Event	Score	Place
Vault		
Bars		
Beam		
Floor		
All Around		

I HAD A NO FALL MEET!

YEAH ME!   WHOOPS

My Team Did Great Too!

My Team Placed

Name	Vault	Bars	Beam	Floor	A.A.

The FUNNIEST thing happened . . .	The HIGHLIGHT was . . .

I Feel like I did . . .	V	UB	BB	FX
THE BEST EVER!				
Better than last time				
OK, The same				
ugh, I'll do better next time				

Photo Op!

For the next meet I'm going to work on . . .

Meet		Date	Level	Age Div

Event	Score	Place
Vault		
Bars		
Beam		
Floor		
All Around		

I HAD A NO FALL MEET!

YEAH ME!   WHOOPS

My Team Did Great Too!

My Team Placed

Name	Vault	Bars	Beam	Floor	A.A.

The FUNNIEST thing happened . . .	The HIGHLIGHT was . . .

I Feel like I did . . .	V	UB	BB	FX
THE BEST EVER!				
Better than last time				
OK, The same				
ugh, I'll do better next time				

Photo Op!

For the next meet I'm going to work on . . .

Meet		Date	Level	Age Div

Event	Score	Place
Vault		
Bars		
Beam		
Floor		
All Around		

I HAD A NO FALL MEET!

YEAH ME!   WHOOPS

My Team Did Great Too!

My Team
Placed

Name	Vault	Bars	Beam	Floor	A.A.

The FUNNIEST thing happened . . .	The HIGHLIGHT was . . .

I Feel like I did . . .	V	UB	BB	FX
THE BEST EVER!				
Better than last time				
OK, The same				
ugh, I'll do better next time				

Photo Op!

For the next meet I'm going to work on . . .

Meet		Date	Level	Age Div

Event	Score	Place
Vault		
Bars		
Beam		
Floor		
All Around		

I HAD A NO FALL MEET!

YEAH ME!   WHOOPS

My Team Did Great Too!

My Team Placed

Name	Vault	Bars	Beam	Floor	A.A.

The FUNNIEST thing happened . . .	The HIGHLIGHT was . . .

I Feel like I did . . .	V	UB	BB	FX
THE BEST EVER!				
Better than last time				
OK, The same				
ugh, I'll do better next time				

Photo Op!

For the next meet I'm going to work on . . .

Meet		Date	Level	Age Div

Event	Score	Place
Vault		
Bars		
Beam		
Floor		
All Around		

I HAD A NO FALL MEET!

YEAH ME!   WHOOPS

My Team Did Great Too!

My Team
Placed

Name	Vault	Bars	Beam	Floor	A.A.

The FUNNIEST thing happened . . .	The HIGHLIGHT was . . .

I Feel like I did . . .	V	UB	BB	FX
THE BEST EVER!				
Better than last time				
OK, The same				
ugh, I'll do better next time				

Photo Op!

For the next meet I'm going to work on . . .

Meet				Date	Level	Age Div

Event	Score	Place
Vault		
Bars		
Beam		
Floor		
All Around		

I HAD A NO FALL MEET!

YEAH ME!   WHOOPS

My Team Did Great Too!

My Team Placed

Name	Vault	Bars	Beam	Floor	A.A.

The FUNNIEST thing happened . . .	The HIGHLIGHT was . . .

I Feel like I did . . .	V	UB	BB	FX
THE BEST EVER!				
Better than last time				
OK, The same				
ugh, I'll do better next time				

Photo Op!

For the next meet I'm going to work on . . .

Meet			Date	Level	Age Div

Event	Score	Place
Vault		
Bars		
Beam		
Floor		
All Around		

I HAD A NO FALL MEET!

YEAH ME!   WHOOPS

My Team
Placed

My Team Did Great Too!

Name	Vault	Bars	Beam	Floor	A.A.

The FUNNIEST thing happened . . .	The HIGHLIGHT was . . .

	V	UB	BB	FX
I Feel like I did . . .				
THE BEST EVER!				
Better than last time				
OK, The same				
ugh, I'll do better next time				

Photo Op!

For the next meet I'm going to work on . . .

Meet		Date	Level	Age Div

Event	Score	Place
Vault		
Bars		
Beam		
Floor		
All Around		

I HAD A NO FALL MEET!

YEAH ME!   WHOOPS

My Team Did Great Too!

My Team Placed

Name	Vault	Bars	Beam	Floor	A.A.

The FUNNIEST thing happened . . .	The HIGHLIGHT was . . .

I Feel like I did . . .	V	UB	BB	FX
THE BEST EVER!				
Better than last time				
OK, The same				
ugh, I'll do better next time				

Photo Op!

For the next meet I'm going to work on . . .

Meet		Date	Level	Age Div

Event	Score	Place
Vault		
Bars		
Beam		
Floor		
All Around		

I HAD A NO FALL MEET!

YEAH ME!   WHOOPS

My Team Did Great Too!

My Team Placed

Name	Vault	Bars	Beam	Floor	A.A.

The FUNNIEST thing happened . . .	The HIGHLIGHT was . . .

I Feel like I did . . .	V	UB	BB	FX
THE BEST EVER!				
Better than last time				
OK, The same				
ugh, I'll do better next time				

Photo Op!

For the next meet I'm going to work on . . .

Meet		Date	Level	Age Div

Event	Score	Place
Vault		
Bars		
Beam		
Floor		
All Around		

I HAD A NO FALL MEET!

YEAH ME!   WHOOPS

My Team Did Great Too!

My Team Placed

Name	Vault	Bars	Beam	Floor	A.A.

The FUNNIEST thing happened . . .	The HIGHLIGHT was . . .

I Feel like I did . . .	V	UB	BB	FX
THE BEST EVER!				
Better than last time				
OK, The same				
ugh, I'll do better next time				

Photo Op!

For the next meet I'm going to work on . . .

Meet		Date	Level	Age Div

Event	Score	Place
Vault		
Bars		
Beam		
Floor		
All Around		

I HAD A NO FALL MEET!

YEAH ME!   WHOOPS

My Team Did Great Too!

My Team Placed

Name	Vault	Bars	Beam	Floor	A.A.

The FUNNIEST thing happened . . .	The HIGHLIGHT was . . .

I Feel like I did . . .	V	UB	BB	FX
THE BEST EVER!				
Better than last time				
OK, The same				
ugh, I'll do better next time				

Photo Op!

For the next meet I'm going to work on . . .

Meet		Date	Level	Age Div

Event	Score	Place
Vault		
Bars		
Beam		
Floor		
All Around		

I HAD A NO FALL MEET!

YEAH ME!   WHOOPS

My Team Did Great Too!   My Team
                                                          Placed

Name	Vault	Bars	Beam	Floor	A.A.

The FUNNIEST thing happened . . .	The HIGHLIGHT was . . .

I Feel like I did . . .	V	UB	BB	FX
THE BEST EVER!				
Better than last time				
OK, The same				
ugh, I'll do better next time				

Photo Op!

For the next meet I'm going to work on . . .

Meet		Date	Level	Age Div

Event	Score	Place
Vault		
Bars		
Beam		
Floor		
All Around		

I HAD A NO FALL MEET!

YEAH ME!   WHOOPS

My Team Placed

My Team Did Great Too!

Name	Vault	Bars	Beam	Floor	A.A.

The FUNNIEST thing happened . . .	The HIGHLIGHT was . . .

I Feel like I did . . .	V	UB	BB	FX
THE BEST EVER!				
Better than last time				
OK, The same				
ugh, I'll do better next time				

Photo Op!

For the next meet I'm going to work on . . .

Meet		Date	Level	Age Div

Event	Score	Place
Vault		
Bars		
Beam		
Floor		
All Around		

I HAD A NO FALL MEET!

YEAH ME!   WHOOPS

My Team Did Great Too!

My Team
Placed

Name	Vault	Bars	Beam	Floor	A.A.

The FUNNIEST thing happened . . .	The HIGHLIGHT was . . .

I Feel like I did . . .	V	UB	BB	FX
THE BEST EVER!				
Better than last time				
OK, The same				
ugh, I'll do better next time				

Photo Op!

For the next meet I'm going to work on . . .

Meet		Date	Level	Age Div

Event	Score	Place
Vault		
Bars		
Beam		
Floor		
All Around		

I HAD A NO FALL MEET!

YEAH ME!   WHOOPS

My Team Did Great Too!

My Team Placed

Name	Vault	Bars	Beam	Floor	A.A.

The FUNNIEST thing happened . . .	The HIGHLIGHT was . . .

I Feel like I did . . .	V	UB	BB	FX
THE BEST EVER!				
Better than last time				
OK, The same				
ugh, I'll do better next time				

Photo Op!

For the next meet I'm going to work on . . .

Meet				Date	Level	Age Div

Event	Score	Place
Vault		
Bars		
Beam		
Floor		
All Around		

I HAD A NO FALL MEET!

YEAH ME!   WHOOPS

My Team Did Great Too!

My Team Placed

Name	Vault	Bars	Beam	Floor	A.A.

The FUNNIEST thing happened . . .	The HIGHLIGHT was . . .

I Feel like I did . . .	V	UB	BB	FX
THE BEST EVER!				
Better than last time				
OK, The same				
ugh, I'll do better next time				

Photo Op!

For the next meet I'm going to work on . . .

Meet			Date	Level	Age Div

Event	Score	Place
Vault		
Bars		
Beam		
Floor		
All Around		

I HAD A NO FALL MEET!

YEAH ME!   WHOOPS

My Team Placed

My Team Did Great Too!

Name	Vault	Bars	Beam	Floor	A.A.

The FUNNIEST thing happened . . .	The HIGHLIGHT was . . .

I Feel like I did . . .	V	UB	BB	FX
THE BEST EVER!				
Better than last time				
OK, The same				
ugh, I'll do better next time				

Photo Op!

For the next meet I'm going to work on . . .

Meet		Date	Level	Age Div

Event	Score	Place
Vault		
Bars		
Beam		
Floor		
All Around		

I HAD A NO FALL MEET!

YEAH ME!   WHOOPS

My Team Did Great Too!

My Team
Placed

Name	Vault	Bars	Beam	Floor	A.A.

The FUNNIEST thing happened . . .	The HIGHLIGHT was . . .

I Feel like I did . . .	V	UB	BB	FX
THE BEST EVER!				
Better than last time				
OK, The same				
ugh, I'll do better next time				

Photo Op!

For the next meet I'm going to work on . . .

Meet			Date	Level	Age Div

Event	Score	Place
Vault		
Bars		
Beam		
Floor		
All Around		

I HAD A NO FALL MEET!

YEAH ME!   WHOOPS

My Team Did Great Too!

My Team Placed

Name	Vault	Bars	Beam	Floor	A.A.

The FUNNIEST thing happened . . .	The HIGHLIGHT was . . .

I Feel like I did . . .	V	UB	BB	FX
THE BEST EVER!				
Better than last time				
OK, The same				
ugh, I'll do better next time				

Photo Op!

For the next meet I'm going to work on . . .

Meet		Date	Level	Age Div

Event	Score	Place
Vault		
Bars		
Beam		
Floor		
All Around		

I HAD A NO FALL MEET!

YEAH ME!   WHOOPS

My Team Did Great Too!

My Team Placed

Name	Vault	Bars	Beam	Floor	A.A.

The FUNNIEST thing happened . . .	The HIGHLIGHT was . . .

I Feel like I did . . .	V	UB	BB	FX
THE BEST EVER!				
Better than last time				
OK, The same				
ugh, I'll do better next time				

Photo Op!

For the next meet I'm going to work on . . .

Meet		Date	Level	Age Div

Event	Score	Place
Vault		
Bars		
Beam		
Floor		
All Around		

I HAD A NO FALL MEET!

YEAH ME!   WHOOPS

My Team Did Great Too!

My Team Placed

Name	Vault	Bars	Beam	Floor	A.A.

The FUNNIEST thing happened . . .	The HIGHLIGHT was . . .

I Feel like I did . . .	V	UB	BB	FX
THE BEST EVER!				
Better than last time				
OK, The same				
ugh, I'll do better next time				

Photo Op!

For the next meet I'm going to work on . . .

Meet		Date	Level	Age Div

Event	Score	Place
Vault		
Bars		
Beam		
Floor		
All Around		

I HAD A NO FALL MEET!

YEAH ME!   WHOOPS

My Team
Placed

My Team Did Great Too!

Name	Vault	Bars	Beam	Floor	A.A.

The FUNNIEST thing happened . . .	The HIGHLIGHT was . . .

I Feel like I did . . .	V	UB	BB	FX
THE BEST EVER!				
Better than last time				
OK, The same				
ugh, I'll do better next time				

Photo Op!

For the next meet I'm going to work on . . .

Meet		Date	Level	Age Div

Event	Score	Place
Vault		
Bars		
Beam		
Floor		
All Around		

I HAD A NO FALL MEET!

YEAH ME!   WHOOPS

My Team Placed

My Team Did Great Too!

Name	Vault	Bars	Beam	Floor	A.A.

The FUNNIEST thing happened . . .	The HIGHLIGHT was . . .

I Feel like I did . . .	V	UB	BB	FX
THE BEST EVER!				
Better than last time				
OK, The same				
ugh, I'll do better next time				

Photo Op!

For the next meet I'm going to work on . . .

Meet		Date	Level	Age Div

Event	Score	Place
Vault		
Bars		
Beam		
Floor		
All Around		

I HAD A NO FALL MEET!

YEAH ME!   WHOOPS

My Team Did Great Too!

My Team Placed

Name	Vault	Bars	Beam	Floor	A.A.

The FUNNIEST thing happened . . .	The HIGHLIGHT was . . .

I Feel like I did . . .	V	UB	BB	FX
THE BEST EVER!				
Better than last time				
OK, The same				
ugh, I'll do better next time				

Photo Op!

For the next meet I'm going to work on . . .

Meet			Date	Level	Age Div

Event	Score	Place
Vault		
Bars		
Beam		
Floor		
All Around		

I HAD A NO FALL MEET!

YEAH ME!   WHOOPS

My Team Did Great Too!

My Team Placed

Name	Vault	Bars	Beam	Floor	A.A.

The FUNNIEST thing happened . . .	The HIGHLIGHT was . . .

I Feel like I did . . .	V	UB	BB	FX
THE BEST EVER!				
Better than last time				
OK, The same				
ugh, I'll do better next time				

Photo Op!

For the next meet I'm going to work on . . .

Meet		Date	Level	Age Div

Event	Score	Place
Vault		
Bars		
Beam		
Floor		
All Around		

I HAD A NO FALL MEET!

YEAH ME!   WHOOPS

My Team Did Great Too!

My Team Placed

Name	Vault	Bars	Beam	Floor	A.A.

The FUNNIEST thing happened . . .	The HIGHLIGHT was . . .

I Feel like I did . . .	V	UB	BB	FX
THE BEST EVER!				
Better than last time				
OK, The same				
ugh, I'll do better next time				

Photo Op!

For the next meet I'm going to work on . . .

Meet		Date	Level	Age Div

Event	Score	Place
Vault		
Bars		
Beam		
Floor		
All Around		

I HAD A NO FALL MEET!

YEAH ME!   WHOOPS

My Team Did Great Too!

My Team Placed

Name	Vault	Bars	Beam	Floor	A.A.

The FUNNIEST thing happened . . .	The HIGHLIGHT was . . .

I Feel like I did . . .	V	UB	BB	FX
THE BEST EVER!				
Better than last time				
OK, The same				
ugh, I'll do better next time				

Photo Op!

For the next meet I'm going to work on . . .

GOALS

Date	Goal	Date Achieved

Oh My! I GOT MY . . . .

Date	Skill	Details

GOALS

Date	Goal	Date Achieved

Oh My! I GOT MY . . . .

Date	Skill	Details

I can beat my high score!

Enter only your highest score.
Each entry should be higher than the last

Vault		Bars		Beam		Floor	
Date	Score	Date	Score	Date	Score	Date	Score

My All Around Scores

Date	Level	Age Division	Score	Place

Bars at a glance

Date	Meet	Level	Score	Place

Vault at a glance

Date	Meet	Level	Score	Place

Floor at a glance

Date	Meet	Level	Score	Place

Beam at a glance

Date	Meet	Level	Score	Place

My 9.0 Chart

Date	Level	Event	Score	Place

My 9.0 Chart

Date	Level	Event	Score	Place

Contacts

Name	Phone	Email	Parents Name

Contacts

Name	Phone	Email	Parents Name

My Gym

Address

Phone Number

Fax

Email

Web address

ALSO FROM DEBORAH SEVILLA &
DREAM BELIEVE ACHIEVE ATHLETICS

ACROBATIC GYMNASTICS

ATHLETE JOURNAL

BASEBALL SCOREBOOK & JOURNAL

COACH EDITIONS WOMEN'S & MEN'S ARTISTIC GYMNASTICS

COLLEGE WORKBOOK

COMPETITIVE DANCE JOURNAL

GYMNASTICS WORKBOOK

MARTIAL ART BELT BOOK & JOURNAL

MARTIAL ARTS COMPETITIVE JOURNAL

MEN'S ARTISTIC GYMNASTICS SCOREBOOKS & JOURNALS

OPTIMISM JOURNAL - 365 DAY JOURNEY TO A BRIGHTER OUTLOOK

OPTIMISM JOUNRAL - YOUTH EDITION

PARENT'S GUIDE COMPETITIVE GYMNASTICS

PRINCESS BALLET WORKBOOK

RHYTHMIC GYMNASTICS

SOFTBALL SCOREBOOK & JOUNAL

WOMEN'S ARTISTIC GYMNASTICS SCOREBOOKS, JOURNALS

AVAILABLE ON AMAZON.COM

WWW.DBAATHLETICS.COM

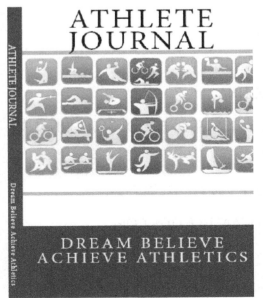
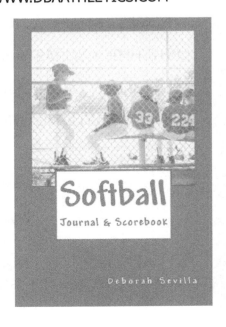